Professional Markdown
for developers

Part 1 : Onboarding

Cheikhna Diouf

Dedication

Dedicated to the reader : May you find happiness.

About the author

Cheikhna Diouf

Tech lead, **IT consultant** (data modeling, software development, computer graphics and UI design).

CEO and founder of the company **EasyGuide.tech**.

Technical writer, speaker and books author.[1]

- **Website: https://easyguide.tech**
- **Blog: https://cheikhnadiouf.com**

Cheikhnadiouf.com

---

[1] **EasyGuide.tech:** https://easyguide.tech

EasyGuide.tech collection

Our project plans to develop a new method and new tools to make the users familiar with any complexe systems as soon as possible.

With **EasyGuide.tech**, beginners should be able to switch quickly between concepts and practices with the aim of improving training , discipline and self-confidence.

- **Website:** https://easyguide.tech
- **Email:** info@easyguide.tech

- **LinkedIn:** https://www.linkedin.com/groups/8230390
- **Meetup:** https://www.meetup.com/fr-FR/easyguide-tech
- **Gitlab project:** https://gitlab.com/easyguide-tech/community

Preface

Practice 10,000 times

This is a modern solution for helping build some rapid, short, easy-to-read, easy-to-understand and **Call-to-action** documents, user guides or manuals.

It is a feature-by-feature practical approach for beginners to help reduce the learning curve of any technical documentations. So any new system or technology will be learned by making repetitive good practices from common and frequent features and patterns with the aim to improve training, discipline and self-confidence.

By analogy, we can compare beginners as athletes who will have to start both physical and mental preparation for sportive competitions and this new tool is ideal for learning easily and quickly the most valuable and useful patterns from real contexts in any domains.

> *"Athletes of all levels grasped what non-athletes sometimes forget: That to master a skill, it's better to practice it 10,000 times--or for 10,000 hours"*
> *- Bruce Lee grasped that practice makes perfect* by Ilan Mochari, Senior writer.

> *"I don't fear the man who has practiced 10,000 kicks. I fear the man who practiced one kick 10,000 times." - Bruce Lee, Martial arts instructor.*

This is a flexible method inspired by Bruce lee philosophy and martial arts technique Jeet Kune Do: 'the art of expressing the human body' :

"Research your own experience. Absorb what is useful, Reject what is useless, Add what is essentially your own." - **Bruce Lee, Martial arts instructor.**

Jeet Kune Do: 'the art of expressing the human body'

Introduction

Theme : About markup languages.

Subject : Here is Markdown, the lightweight markup language with plain text formatting syntax.

Interest : Easy-to-read, Easy-to-write and Easy-to-code markup language for developers with the aim to help them deploy quickly some dynamic and robust documents.

Plan :

- Tools and Rules

  For quick start

  - Features
  - Requirements
  - Setup
  - Usage
  - Rules

- Rapid text formatting

  For team communication

  - Headings
  - Style
  - Strikethrough
  - Link
  - Lists
  - Image
  - Quote
  - BlockQuote
  - Inline code
  - Block code
  - Horizontal Rule
  - Footnote
  - Definition list
  - TOC generation (Table Of Contents)

- Illustration widgets

  For rich documentations

  - Table
  - Task list
  - Inline HTML for advanced widgets
  - Form
  - Video
  - Diagram snippets (with PlantUML)

- Multiple export formats

  For sharing

  - Pandoc, the swiss-army knife
  - Recommended Addons for Markdown and Pandoc

Table of contents

I.   Tools and Rules

For quick start

<table>
<tr><td align="center">(?) User note:</td></tr>
</table>

Your notes from your own practices :

....
....
....
....

1. Features

Markdown logo

Markdown is a **markup language** made for rapid and easy writing of document by formatting elements with only plain text content.

Markdown was developed in 2004 by John Gruber in collaboration with Aaron Swartz. Gruber wrote the first markdown-to-html converter in Perl, and it soon became widely used in websites. By 2014 there were dozens of implementations in many languages.

(i) Info note:

No need of rich visual text software like Microsoft Word or others, the text in Markdown files can be edited with a simple text editor and can be read even if it isn't rendered or previewed by a Markdown application.

(?) User note:

Your notes from your own practices :

....
....
....
....

Glossary

Markup language

According to wikipedia[2]   - "In computer text processing, a markup language is a system for annotating a document in a way that is syntactically distinguishable from the text. The idea and terminology evolved from the"marking up" of paper manuscripts (i.e., the revision instructions by editors), which is traditionally written with a red or blue pencil on authors' manuscripts. In digital media, this "blue pencil instruction text" was replaced by tags, which indicate what the parts of the document are, rather than details of how they might be shown on some display."

Markdown application

According to wikipedia[3]   - "It is a tool with a Markdown processor (also commonly referred to as a "parser" or an "implementation") to take the Markup-formatted text and output it to HTML format. At that point, your document can be viewed in a web browser or combined with a style sheet and printed."

---

[2] Wikipedia : https://en.wikipedia.org/wiki/Markdown
[3] Wikipedia : https://en.wikipedia.org/wiki/Markdown

2. Implementations

Syntax variations

There are many different implementations also called **Markdown Flavors** [4], different syntax variations of the markdown parser. We choose in our examples one of the most standard and popular extended implementations: the **CommonMark**[5] and the **GitHub-flavored Markdown**[6]

* **https://commonmark.org/**
* **https://guides.github.com/features/mastering-markdown/**.

---

[4] **GitHub Flavored Markdown:** https://guides.github.com/features/mastering-markdown/

[5] **CommonMark:** https://commonmark.org/

[6] **GitHub Flavored Markdown:** https://guides.github.com/features/mastering-markdown/

(i) Info note:

Here a list of markdown applications that you can use :

- **CommonMark** [7] (most standard specification)
- CriticMarkup
- Discount
- DocFX
- ExtraMark
- Ghost's Markdown/Haunted Markdown
- **GitHub Flavored Markdown**[8] (Current choice for our extended examples)
- GitLab Flavored Markdown (with login)
- Haroopad Flavored Markdown
- iA Writer's Markdown
- Kramdown
- Leanpub Flavored Markdown
- Litedown
- Lunamark
- Madoko
- Markdown
- Markdown 2
- Markdown Extra
- Markdown-it
- Markua
- Maruku

---

[7] **CommonMark:** https://commonmark.org/
[8] **GitHub Flavored Markdown:** https://guides.github.com/features/mastering-markdown/

- MultiMarkdown
- Pandoc's Markdown
- PHP Markdown Extra Extended
- Python Markdown
- Redcarpet
- Remarkable
- Rhythmus
- Scholarly Markdown
- Showdown
- StackOverflow's Markdown
- Taiga Markdown
- Trello's Markdown
- vfmd
- Xcode/Swift Playgrounds Markup

(i) Info note:

There is further flavors to add to this list, source from the the Markdown GitHub Organization [9] >
https://github.com/markdown/markdown.github.com/wiki/Imple mentations

---

[9] **Wikipedia:** https://en.wikipedia.org/wiki/Markdown

(i) Info note:

The very useful tool, **Babelmark 2** [10], has been provided by John MacFarlane to compare the output of various implementations of John Gruber's markdown syntax for plain text documents.
Babelmark 2 - https://johnmacfarlane.net/babelmark2/faq.html

(?) User note:

Your notes from your own practices :

....
....
....
....

---

[10] **Babelmark 2** https://johnmacfarlane.net/babelmark2/faq.html

Requirements

1. A Markdown application editor for developers : Like **Microsoft Visual Code** (and its extension **Markdown Preview Enhanced**) or any similar Markdown application editor with similar preview extension.
2. A diagram plain text parser : **PlantUML**[11] with **Graphviz** and Java (JRE)
3. A multiple export formats library : **Pandoc**[12] (see last chapter for advanced setup instructions)
4. A **Markdown parser library** implemented in your programming language There are libraries available in a number of languages and a quick search online reveals parser libraries for java, c#, python, javascript, php, ruby, haskell, etc.

---

[11] **PlantUML** https://github.com/plantuml/plantuml

[12] **Pandoc** https://github.com/jgm/pandoc

> ## (i) Info note:
>
> For simple and common business use cases, Markdown just needs some less technical **document authoring applications** such as those listed below [13]:
>
> - on Windows ghostwriter or Markdown Monster
> - on Linux ReText or ghostwriter
> - on Web Dillinger or StackEdit
> - on Mac MacDown, iA Writer, or Marked
> - on iOS / Android iA Writer

---

[13] **Markdownguide:** https://www.markdownguide.org

(i) Info note:

Markdown Parser library The original implementation was written in Perl. Today, there are implementations in most popular languages :

• **JavaScript:**

- CommonMark

- Marked

- Markdown-it

- Remarkable

- Showdown

• **Ruby:**

- Github Flavored Markup

- Kramdown

- Maruku

- Redcarpet

• **PHP:**

- Cebe Markdown

- Ciconia

- Parsedown

- PHP Markdown Extended

• **Python:**

- Python Markdown

> ## (i) Info note:
>
> The **Markdown mark** graphic files library can be found here: **https://github.com/dcurtis/markdown-mark** Use this mark to identify Markdown.
>
> It can be used to identify user input areas which support Markdown-compiled HTML output or to identify general Markdown support.

3. Setup

(?) User note:
Your notes from your own practices : ....

Download and install Microsoft Visual Code editor

.

a free code editor with some useful extensions for Markdown professionnal uses.

Microsoft visual code - https://code.visualstudio.com/

Recommended Markdown extensions for Microsoft visual code editor**

- First, **How to Install Useful extensions** for Microsoft Visual Code:

    1. On the toolbar in the left screen, click on Extensions icon button
    2. Then type the name of the extension
    3. Select in the result list this extension
    4. Then click on Install button

- **the** Markdown Preview Enhanced **extension** Markdown Preview Enhanced is an extension that provides you with many useful functionalities such as automatic scroll sync, math typesetting, mermaid, **PlantUML**, **Pandoc**, PDF export, code chunk, presentation writer. A lot of its ideas are inspired by Markdown Preview Plus and RStudio Markdown. Link: https://marketplace.visualstudio.com/items?itemName=shd101 wyy.markdown-preview-enhanced

- **The** Markdownlint **extension** Markdownlint is a Visual Studio Code extension that includes a library of rules to encourage standards and consistency for Markdown files. It is powered by markdownlint for Node.js which is based on markdownlint for

Ruby. Link:
https://marketplace.visualstudio.com/items?itemName=DavidAnson.vscode-markdownlint

---

(i) Info note:

Rules can be enabled, disabled, and customized by creating a JSON file named .markdownlint.json (or .markdownlintrc) or a YAML file named .markdownlint.yaml (or .markdownlint.yml) in any directory of a project.

The rules defined by .markdownlint{.json,.yaml,.yml,rc} apply to Markdown files in the same directory and any sub-directories without their own .markdownlint{.json,yaml,.yml,rc}.

The default rule is applied first, then keys are processed in order from top to bottom with later values overriding earlier ones.

---

console.log Example config in json

```
{
  "default": true,
  "MD003": { "style": "atx_closed" },
  "MD007": { "indent": 4 },
  "no-hard-tabs": false,
  "whitespace": false
}
```

```
Example config in yaml

default: true
MD003:
  style: "atx_closed"
MD007:
  indent: 4
no-hard-tabs: false
whitespace: false
```

A library to render graph diagrams : PlantUML and Graphviz

https://plantuml.com/en/ PlantUML is a component that allows to quickly write :

- Sequence diagram
- Usecase diagram
- Class diagram
- Activity diagram (here is the legacy syntax)
- Component diagram
- State diagram
- Object diagram
- Deployment diagram
- Timing diagram

The following non-UML diagrams are also supported:

- Wireframe graphical interface
- Archimate diagram
- Specification and Description Language (SDL)
- Ditaa diagram
- Gantt diagram
- MindMap diagram
- Work Breakdown Structure diagram
- Mathematic with AsciiMath or JLaTeXMath notation

- Entity Relationship diagram

Images can be generated in PNG, in SVG or in LaTeX format. It is also possible to generate ASCII art diagrams (only for sequence diagrams).

- **Example:**

> ```plantuml
>
> Bob->Alice : hello
>
> ```

- **Output:**

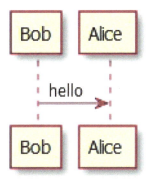

To download and install PlantUML:
https://plantuml.com/en/starting

You need these things to run PlantUML locally:

- **Java** The object programming language
  https://www.java.com/en/download/
- **Graphviz** (optional if you only need sequence diagrams and activity (beta) diagrams) Graphviz is open source graph visualization software **http://graphviz.org/download/**

Installed the above? Then simply download plantuml.jar and run it to open PlantUML's graphical user interface. There is no need to unpack or install anything.

> ## (i) Info note:
>
> On Microsoft Windows OS, declare it by adding the application file path to environment variable system called PATH. plantuml in PATH which launches PlantUML jar Example path :
> C:\plantuml\plantuml.jar

A Markdown parser library implemented in any programming language : Markdown-it

Here you can find for example a JavaScript-implementation of Markdown : Markdown-it and node-pandoc It can be used client side (in the browser) or server side (with Node.js).

Markdown-it: Markdown parser done right. Fast and easy to extend.

Live demo : **https://markdown-it.github.io**

- Follows the CommonMark spec + adds syntax extensions & sugar (URL autolinking, typographer).

  http://spec.commonmark.org/

- Configurable syntax! You can add new rules and even replace existing ones.

- High speed.

- **Safe** by default. **https://github.com/markdown-it/markdown-it/tree/master/docs/security.md**

- Community-written plugins and **other packages** on npm.

  - **https://www.npmjs.org/browse/keyword/markdown-it-plugin**

  - **https://www.npmjs.org/browse/keyword/markdown-it**

Install with node.js or bower:

- **Example:**

```
npm install markdown-it --save
bower install markdown-it --save
```

Markdown-it plugins:

- **markdown-it-plantuml** Plugin for creating block-level uml diagrams for markdown-it markdown parser.
https://www.npmjs.com/package/markdown-it-plantuml

- **markdown-it-pandoc** Package bundling a few markdown-it plugins to approximate pandoc flavoured markdown
https://www.npmjs.com/package/markdown-it-pandoc

Download the example code files for this book

You can download the example code files for this book **from your account at EasyGuide.tech**.

You can download the code files by following these steps:

1. Log in or register at **https://www.easyguide.tech**
2. Select the name of the book in the Search box
3. Click on **Code Download** button.
4. Follow the onscreen instructions.

Once the file is downloaded, please make sure that you unzip or extract the folder using the latest version of:

- WinRAR/7-Zip **for Windows**
- Zipeg/iZip/UnRarX **for Mac**
- 7-Zip/PeaZip **for Linux**

4. Usage

<table>
<tr><td align="center">(?) User note:</td></tr>
<tr><td>Your notes from your own practices :</td></tr>
<tr><td>..</td></tr>
<tr><td>..</td></tr>
<tr><td>..</td></tr>
<tr><td>..</td></tr>
</table>

Edit

1. Create a Markdown file using a text editor or a dedicated Markdown application editor. The file should have an .md or .markdown extension.

2. Edit this plain text document

Render

1. Open the Markdown file in a Markdown application.

2. Use the Markdown application to convert the Markdown file to an HTML document.

3. View the HTML file in a web browser or use the Markdown application to preview or convert it to another file format, like PDF.

4. See chapter **Export to Multiple formats** to learn more about available output formats.

Implement Markdown parser library in your code

1. Open the Markdown file in a Markdown application.

2. Use the Markdown application to convert the Markdown file to an HTML document.

3. View the HTML file in a web browser or use the Markdown application to preview or convert it to another file format, like PDF.

4. See chapter **Export to Multiple formats** to learn more about available output formats.

- **Example with Markdown-it parser** implemented in Javascript
  :

```
// node.js, "classic" way:
var MarkdownIt = require("markdown-it"),
  md = new MarkdownIt();
var result = md.render("# markdown-it rulezz!");

// node.js, the same, but with sugar:
var md = require("markdown-it")();
var result = md.render("# markdown-it rulezz!");

// browser without AMD, added to "window" on script load
// Note, there is no dash in "markdownit".
var md = window.markdownit();
var result = md.render("# markdown-it rulezz!");

// Single line rendering, without paragraph wrap:
var md = require("markdown-it")();
var result = md.renderInline("__markdown-it__ rulezz!");
```

- **Example with Markdown-it Plugins load** implemented in
  Javascript

```
// Plugins load
var md = require('markdown-it')()
        .use(plugin1)
        .use(plugin2, opts, ...)
        .use(plugin3);
```

5. Rules

(?) User note:

Your notes from your own practices :

....

....

....

....

Syntax Rules

The CommonMark specification standardizes parsers - but not authors. Below is an example of Markdown syntax standards based on source from **Markdown-Lint**. A Node.js style checker and lint tool for Markdown/CommonMark files.
https://github.com/DavidAnson/markdownlint

Rules / Aliases: This is a resume list of all rules, what they are checking for. Any rule whose heading is struck through is deprecated, but still provided for backward-compatibility.[14]

- **[MD001]** *heading-increment/header-increment* - Heading levels should only increment by one level at a time

- **[MD002]** *first-heading-h1/first-header-h1* - First heading should be a top level heading

- **[MD003]** *heading-style/header-style* - Heading style

- **[MD004]** *ul-style* - Unordered list style

- **[MD005]** *list-indent* - Inconsistent indentation for list items at the same level

- **[MD006]** *ul-start-left* - Consider starting bulleted lists at the beginning of the line

- **[MD007]** *ul-indent* - Unordered list indentation

- **[MD009]** *no-trailing-spaces* - Trailing spaces

- **[MD010]** *no-hard-tabs* - Hard tabs

- **[MD011]** *no-reversed-links* - Reversed link syntax

- **[MD012]** *no-multiple-blanks* - Multiple consecutive blank lines

---

[14] **MarkdownLint:** https://github.com/DavidAnson/markdownlint

- **[MD013]** *line-length* - Line length

- **[MD014]** *commands-show-output* - Dollar signs used before commands without showing output

- **[MD018]** *no-missing-space-atx* - No space after hash on atx style heading

- **[MD019]** *no-multiple-space-atx* - Multiple spaces after hash on atx style heading

- **[MD020]** *no-missing-space-closed-atx* - No space inside hashes on closed atx style heading

- **[MD021]** *no-multiple-space-closed-atx* - Multiple spaces inside hashes on closed atx style heading

- **[MD022]** *blanks-around-headings/blanks-around-headers* - Headings should be surrounded by blank lines

- **[MD023]** *heading-start-left/header-start-left* - Headings must start at the beginning of the line

- **[MD024]** *no-duplicate-heading/no-duplicate-header* - Multiple headings with the same content

- **[MD025]** *single-title/single-h1* - Multiple top level headings in the same document

- **[MD026]** *no-trailing-punctuation* - Trailing punctuation in heading

- **[MD027]** *no-multiple-space-blockquote* - Multiple spaces after blockquote symbol

- **[MD028]** *no-blanks-blockquote* - Blank line inside blockquote

- **[MD029]** *ol-prefix* - Ordered list item prefix

- **[MD030]** *list-marker-space* - Spaces after list markers

- **[MD031]** *blanks-around-fences* - Fenced code blocks should be surrounded by blank lines

- **[MD032]** *blanks-around-lists* - Lists should be surrounded by blank lines

- **[MD033]** *no-inline-html* - Inline HTML

- **[MD034]** *no-bare-urls* - Bare URL used

- **[MD035]** *hr-style* - Horizontal rule style

- **[MD036]** *no-emphasis-as-heading/no-emphasis-as-header* - Emphasis used instead of a heading

- **[MD037]** *no-space-in-emphasis* - Spaces inside emphasis markers

- **[MD038]** *no-space-in-code* - Spaces inside code span elements

- **[MD039]** *no-space-in-links* - Spaces inside link text

- **[MD040]** *fenced-code-language* - Fenced code blocks should have a language specified

- **[MD041]** *first-line-heading/first-line-h1* - First line in file should be a top level heading

- **[MD042]** *no-empty-links* - No empty links

- **[MD043]** *required-headings/required-headers* - Required heading structure

- **[MD044]** *proper-names* - Proper names should have the correct capitalization

- **[MD045]

- **[MD046]** *code-block-style* - Code block style

- **[MD047]** *single-trailing-newline* - Files should end with a single newline character

- **[MD048]** *code-fence-style* - Code fence style

See **Markdown Lint Author Rules** online for more details.
https://github.com/DavidAnson/markdownlint

Parser Rules

To analyse or validate any Markdown applications See the CommonMark standards specifications and resources below:

> ### (i) Info note:
>
> Why the CommonMark specification ? [15] "Because there is no unambiguous spec, implementations have diverged considerably over the last 10 years.
>
> As a result, users are often surprised to find that a document that renders one way on one system (say, a GitHub wiki) renders differently on another (say, converting to docbook using Pandoc).
>
> To make matters worse, because nothing in Markdown counts as a "syntax error," the divergence often isn't discovered right away.
>
> CommonMark suggest a standard, unambiguous syntax specification for Markdown, along with a suite of comprehensive tests to validate Markdown implementations against this specification.
>
> We believe this is necessary, even essential, for the future of Markdown." - Source : **https://commonmark.org/**

- **The CommonMark specification**.
  https://spec.commonmark.org

- **Reference implementation and validation test suite** on GitHub. **https://code.commonmark.org**

- **Live testing tool** powered by the reference implementation.
  https://spec.commonmark.org/dingus

---

[15] **CommonMark:** https://commonmark.org/

II.   Rapid Text formatting

For team communication

(?) User note:

Your notes from your own practices :

....
....
....
....

1. Headings

Add Heading title

1. Type # character to interpret this line as a title
2. Type any text
3. Code source

```
# Heading H1
```

4. Then preview:

Heading H1

Alternatively use underlines for H1 and H2 heading titles

1. Type = underline characters (at least 3) to interpret above line as a title H1
2. Code source

```
# Heading H1
```

3. Type - underline characters (at least 3) to interpret above line as a title H2
4. Code source

```
## Heading H2
```

5. Then preview:

Heading H1

Heading H2

Add deeper headings and sub titles

1. Type code source below. Multiple ## in a row to render smaller heading sizes.

> *# Heading H1: previewed as an <h1> tag*
>
> *## Heading H2: previewed as an <h2> tag*
>
> *### Heading H3: previewed as an <h3> tag*
>
> *#### Heading H4: previewed as an <h4> tag*
>
> *##### Heading H5: previewed as an <h5> tag*
>
> *###### Heading H6: previewed as an <h6> tag*

2. Then preview:

Heading H1: previewed as an <h1> tag

Heading H2: previewed as an <h2> tag

Heading H3: previewed as an <h3> tag

Heading H4: previewed as an <h4> tag

Heading H5: previewed as an <h5> tag

Heading H6: previewed as an <h6> tag

2. Styles

<table>
<tr><td colspan="1" align="center">(?) User note:</td></tr>
</table>

(?) User note:
Your notes from your own practices :
....
....
....
....

Italic emphasis

1. Type * asterisk or _ underscore characters for italic style
2. Type code source below

previewed in italic
also previewed in italic

3. Then preview:

previewed in italic

also previewed in italic

Bold emphasis

1. Type ** asterisk or __double underscore characters for italic style
2. Type code source below

> **previewed in bold**
> **also previewed in bold**

3. Then preview:

previewed in bold

also previewed in bold

Strikethrough

1. Type code source below (specify the language name)

> ~~This line is a strikethrough~~

2. Then preview:

~~This line is a strikethrough~~

3. Link

<table>
<tr><td align="center">(?) User note:</td></tr>
</table>

Your notes from your own practices :

....
....
....
....

Default

1. Type code source below

[link to EasyGuide.tech](https://easyguide.tech)

2. Then preview:

link to EasyGuide.tech

Reference link by text label

1. Type code source below

[Label link EasyGuide.tech]

2. and Type this code source at footer

[label link easyguide.tech]: http://easyguide.tech

3. Then preview:

Label link EasyGuide.tech

Reference link by ID number

1. Type code source below

   [Reference link to EasyGuide.tech][1]

2. and Type this code source at footer

   [1]: http://easyguide.tech

3. Then preview:

   Reference link to EasyGuide.tech

Reference menu link by hashtag

1. Type this code source

   # EasyGuide.tech

2. and Type code source below

   [Hastag link to EasyGuide.tech](#link-to-easyguide)

3. Then preview:

   EasyGuide.tech

   Hashtag link to EasyGuide.tech

Reference custom ID link

1. Type code source below

   # EasyGuide.tech {#custom-id-link}

2. And Type code source below

   [Custom ID link to EasyGuide.tec][#custom-id-link]

3. Then preview:

   EasyGuide.tech

   Custom ID link to EasyGuide.tech

4. Lists

(?) User note:

Your notes from your own practices :

....

....

....

....

Unordered list

1. Type code source below

```
- Items 1
  - Items 1.2
    - Item 1.2.1
    - Item 1.2.2
```

2. Then preview:

- Items 1

    – Items 1.2

        • Item 1.2.1

        • Item 1.2.2

ordered list

1.   Type code source below

```
1. Item 1
2. Item 2
3. Item 3
   1. Item 3.1
   2. Item 3.2
```

2.   Then preview:

1.   Item 1
2.   Item 2
3.   Item 3
    1.   Item 3.1
    2.   Item 3.2

6. Image

Default

1. Type code source below

   ![logo image](assets/images/logo.png "Logo title text")

2. Then preview:

logo image

(!) Warning note:

Resize image : compatibility issue Depending on Markdown applications, you can resize the image by adding more expressions like this:

- =WIDTHxHEIGHT or =WIDTH after the URL of the graphic file

- {width=100%} or {width=300px}.

- you can directly replace ![title](image-url) with an inline html
<img src="image-url" width="200" height="200">

Reference image link by ID text

1. Type code source below

   ![EasyGuide.tech Logo][logo]

2. And Type this code source at footer

   [logo]: assets/images/logo.png "Logo title text"

3. Then preview:

EasyGuide.tech Logo

7. Quote

Default

1. Type code source below

   > *Rendered as quote.*

2. Then preview:

   Rendered as quote.

(?) User note:

Your notes from your own practices :

....
....
....
....

---

8. BlockQuote

Default

1. Type code source below

> *Rendered as line quote 1.*
> *Rendered as line quote 2.*

2. Then preview:

Rendered as line quote 1.
Rendered as line quote 2.

(?) User note:

Your notes from your own practices :

....
....
....
....

9. Inline code

Default

1. Type code source below

> *the one star character delimiters will be previewed in html as the `<strong></strong>` tags*

2. Then preview:

the one star character delimiters will be previewed in html as the `<strong></strong>` tags

---

(?) User note:

Your notes from your own practices :

....
....
....
....

---

10.   Block code

Default

1. Type code source below

    ```
    ```
    if (isAwesome){
      return true
    }
    ```
    ```

2. Then preview:

```
if (isAwesome){

    return true

}
```

(?) User note:

Your notes from your own practices :

....
....
....
....

With syntax highlighting

1. Type code source below (specify the language name)

    ```js
    if (isAwesome){
      return true
    }
    ```

2. Then preview:

    ```
    if (isAwesome){
       return true
    }
    ```

(?) User note:

Your notes from your own practices :

....

....

....

....

---

11.   Horizontal Rule

Default

1. Type code source below

    ```
    ---
    ```

2. Then preview:

12.   **Footnote**

Default

1.   Type code source below

> *Here's a sentence with a footnote. [^1]*
>
> *[^1]: Footnote.*

2.   Then preview:

Here's a sentence with a footnote. [16]

(?) User note:
Your notes from your own practices :
....
....
....
....

---

[16] Footnote example in markdown.

13.   Definition list

Default

1.   Type code source below

> *term*
> *: definition*

2.   Then preview:

term

    definition

(?) User note:

Your notes from your own practices :

....
....
....
....

---

14.   TOC generation (Table Of Contents)

Default

1. Use any utils to generate automatically a markdown menu also called a table of contents (TOC)

2. Example with **Markdown Preview Enhanced** [17] extension :

    1. You can press cmd-shift-p
       then choose Markdown Preview Enhanced: Create Toc to create automatically the table of contents.
       Multiple TOCs can be created.
       To exclude a heading from the TOC, append {ignore=true} after your heading.
    2. The TOC will be updated when you save the markdown file.
       You need to keep the preview open to get TOC updated.
       Read more on this tutorial link :
       https://shd101wyy.github.io/markdown-preview-enhanced/#/toc

---

[17] **Markdown Preview Enhanced** https://github.com/shd101wyy/markdown-preview-enhanced

```
<!-- @import "[TOC]" {cmd="toc" depthFrom=1 depthTo=2
orderedList=false } -->

<!-- code_chunk_output -->

- [Introduction](#introduction)
- [Chapter 1](#chapter-1)
  - [Sub chapter 1](#sub-chapter-1)
  - [Sub chapter 2](#sub-chapter2)
- [Chapter 2](#chapter-2)

<!-- /code_chunk_output -->
```

3. Then preview:

- **Introduction**

- **Chapter 1**

    – **Sub chapter 1**

    – **Sub chapter 2**

- **Chapter 2**

(?) User note:
Your notes from your own practices :
....
....
....
....

III.   Illustration widgets

For rich documentations

(?) User note:

Your notes from your own practices :

....
....
....
....

1. Table

Default

1. Type code source below

head left	title centered	title right
row	value	value
another row	another value	another value

2. Colons are used to align columns:

   – **left or none:** :---- or ----

   – **right:** ----:

   – **centered:** :----:

3. Then preview:

head left	title centered	title right
row	value	value
another row	another value	another value

2. Task list

Default

1. Type code source below

    > - [x] this is a complete item
    > - [ ] this is an incomplete item

2. Then preview:

☑ this is a complete item

☐ this is an incomplete item

3. Inline HTML for advanced widgets

Like google map, form, video etc.

(?) User note:
Your notes from your own practices :
....
....
....
....

Default

1. Type **google map** code source below directly in html (example from **embedgooglemap.net**)

```
<div class="mapouter">
  <div class="gmap_canvas">

<iframe width="400" height="400" id="gmap_canvas"
src="https://maps.google.com/maps?q=arc%20de%20triomp
he&t=k&z=17&ie=UTF8&iwloc=&output=embed"
      frameborder="0" scrolling="no" marginheight="0"
marginwidth="0"></iframe>
</div>
```

2. Then preview:

4. Form

(?) User note:
Your notes from your own practices :
....
....
....
....

Default

1. Type code source below directly in html

```
<form action="/action_page">
  <input type="text" placeholder="Enter input message here"
/>
  <input type="date" value="12/01/2012" />
  <select>
    <option value="value 1"> label item 1</option>
    <option value="value 2"> label item 2</option>
  </select>
  <textarea rows="4" cols="50">
It is so easy to break down and destroy. The heroes are
those who make peace and build - Nelson
Mandela</textarea>
  <input type="submit" value="submit" />
</form>
```

2. Then preview:

5. Video

Your notes from your own practices :

....

....

....

....

Default

1. Type code source below directly in html

```
<a
href="http://www.youtube.com/watch?feature=player_embed
ded&v=9XTcdAmmnVk"
   target="_blank">
   <img
      src="http://img.youtube.com/vi/9XTcdAmmnVk/0.jpg"
      alt="We are the world: USA for Africa"
      width="560"
      height="315" />
</a>
```

2. Then preview:

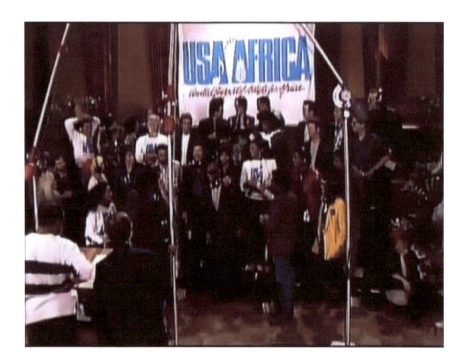

Video by image markup

1. Type code source below

> *[![We are the world: USA for Africa](http://img.youtube.com/vi/9XTcdAmmnVk/0.jpg)](http://www.youtube.com/watch?v=9XTcdAmmnVk)*

2. Then preview:

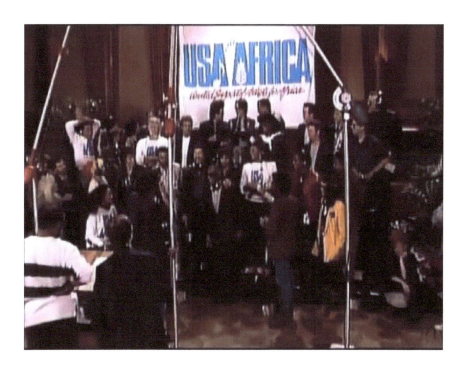

6. Diagram snippets (with PlantUML)

PlantUML[18] is a graph addon for markdown scripted diagrams and icons (amazon, font awesome, etc.)

(i) Info note:

https://plantuml.com

Easily create beautiful UML Diagrams from simple textual description.
There are also numerous kind of available diagrams.
It's also possible to export images in PNG, LaTeX, EPS, SVG.

PlantUML is a component that allows to quickly write :

- Sequence diagram
- Usecase diagram
- Class diagram
- Activity diagram (here is the legacy syntax)
- Component diagram
- State diagram
- Object diagram
- Deployment diagram
- Timing diagram

The following non-UML diagrams are also supported:

- Wireframe graphical interface
- Archimate diagram
- Specification and Description Language (SDL)
- Ditaa diagram
- Gantt diagram
- MindMap diagram
- Work Breakdown Structure diagram

---

[18] **PlantUML** https://github.com/plantuml/plantuml

- Mathematic with AsciiMath or JLaTeXMath notation
- Entity Relationship diagram

(!) Warning note:

In our example codes here we illustrate some **more complete and more advanced diagram samples** than the plantUML website.

Useful snippets that you can customize for your work but if you need more simple and basic examples, you can get them on plantUML website : **https://plantuml.com**

(?) User note:

Your notes from your own practices :

....
....
....
....

Context snippet for deployment or context diagrams

1. Type code source below (a full example of software
   architecture)

```
```plantuml

'SETTINGS
'---
'scale 720 width
left to right direction

'Title custom style
skinparam titleBorderRoundCorner 0
skinparam titleBorderThickness 1
skinparam titleBackgroundColor red
skinparam titleFontColor white
skinparam titleFontSize 24

'legend custom style
skinparam legendBorderRoundCorner 0
skinparam legendBorderThickness 0
skinparam legendFontSize 14
skinparam legendFontColor white
skinparam legendBackgroundColor darkGrey

'HEADER
'---
title
<font color=white> Architecture overview : Deployment
diagram </font>
 end title

legend top right
<font color=red>Objective : </font> Overview of the
system's architecture.
```
```

```
end legend


'BODY
'---


node "Personal computer" as Pc <<device>> {
   node "Web browser" as WebBrowser <<software>> {
      component "Angular frontend" as Angular <<web-
app>>
   }
}



   node "Web server" as WebServer <<device>> {
      component "Java backend" as Java <<web-api>>
   }


   cloud "Cloud service" as CloudService <<device>>
#darkGrey {
      artifact "Rest web service" as WebService <<web-api>>
   }

   database "Database server" as Database <<device>> #red
{
      storage "MySql data store" as MySql <<storage>>
   }

   Angular --(0--- Java : <font color=red>HTTP REST </font>
<<protocol>>
   Java --(0-- MySql : <font color=red>TCP/IP</font>
<<protocol>>
   Java --(0-- WebService : <font color=red>HTTP
REST</font> <<protocol>>


   ...
```

2. Then preview:

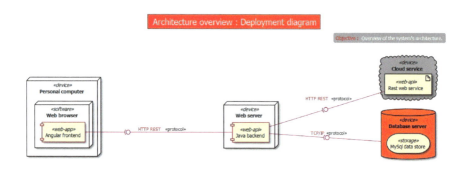

Infrastructure snippet for package, component, folder or file diagrams

1. Type code source below (a full example of application structure folder with angular framework)

```plantuml
'SETTINGS
'---
'scale 720 width

allow_mixing


'HEADER
'---
title
<font color=white> Frontend : Package/component </font>
end title

legend top right
<font color=red>Objective : </font> Overview of the
system's folders/files.
end legend

'Title custom style
skinparam titleBorderRoundCorner 0
skinparam titleBorderThickness 1
skinparam titleBackgroundColor red
skinparam titleFontColor white
skinparam titleFontSize 24

'legend custom style
skinparam legendBorderRoundCorner 0
skinparam legendBorderThickness 0
skinparam legendFontSize 14
```

```
skinparam legendFontColor white
skinparam legendBackgroundColor darkGrey


'BODY
'---

package angular_core as "Angular Core" {
}

angular_core -right-> module

package module as "feature.module.ts" {
agent "feature.interface.ts" as interface
agent "feature.model.ts" as model
agent "feature.service.ts" as service
agent "feature-routing.module.ts" as route
route --> component

package component  as "feature.component.ts" {
agent "feature.template.html" as template
agent "feature.style.scss" as style
agent "feature.controller" as controller
}



template --> style
template --> controller
model --> controller
service --> model
controller --> service
service <-- interface


}
...
```

2. Then preview:

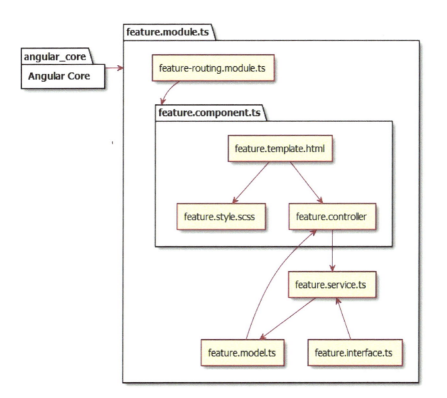

Feature/Relation snippet for Entity-Relation or activity diagrams

1. Type code source below

```
```plantuml
'SETTINGS
'---
'scale 720 width
'left to right direction

'Title custom style
skinparam titleBorderRoundCorner 0
skinparam titleBorderThickness 1
skinparam titleBackgroundColor red
skinparam titleFontColor white
skinparam titleFontSize 24

'legend custom style
skinparam legendBorderRoundCorner 0
skinparam legendBorderThickness 0
skinparam legendFontSize 14
skinparam legendFontColor white
skinparam legendBackgroundColor darkGrey

'HEADER
'---
title
<font color=white> Example : Activity diagram </font>
end title

legend top right
<font color=red>Objective : </font> Overview of the
system's activity
end legend
```
```

```
'BODY
'___

start
:ClickServlet.handleRequest();
:new page;
if (Page.onSecurityCheck) then (true)
  :Page.onInit();
  if (isForward?) then (no)
  :Process controls;
  if (continue processing?) then (no)
    stop
  endif

  if (isPost?) then (yes)
    :Page.onPost();
  else (no)
    :Page.onGet();
  endif
  :Page.onRender();
  endif
else (false)
endif

if (do redirect?) then (yes)
  :redirect process;
else
  if (do forward?) then (yes)
  :Forward request;
  else (no)
  :Render page template;
  endif
endif

stop

```
```
```

2. then preview:

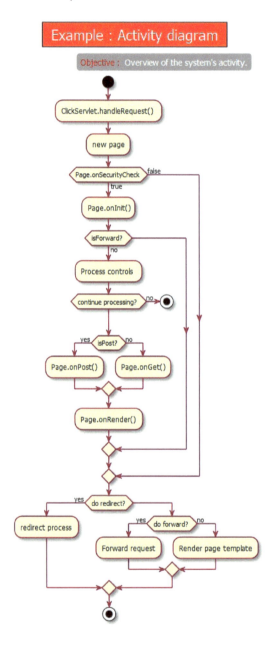

Structure snippet for class diagrams

1. Type code source below (a full example of class diagram based on Angular framework)

```plantuml

'SETTINGS
'---
'scale 720 width
left to right direction

'Title custom style
skinparam titleBorderRoundCorner 0
skinparam titleBorderThickness 1
skinparam titleBackgroundColor red
skinparam titleFontColor white
skinparam titleFontSize 24

'legend custom style
skinparam legendBorderRoundCorner 0
skinparam legendBorderThickness 0
skinparam legendFontSize 14
skinparam legendFontColor white
skinparam legendBackgroundColor darkGrey

'HEADER
'---
title
<font color=white> Frontend : Class diagram </font>
end title

legend top right
<font color=red>Objective : </font> Overview of the
system's structure.
 end legend
```

```
'BODY
'---
class "feature-routing.module" as featureRouterModule

class "featureComponent" as featureComponent{
    currentModel: FeatureModel
    service: FeatureService
    ---
    ngOnInit()
}
class "featureModel" as featureModel
interface "IDataJson" as IDataJson #lightGreen
class "featureService" as featureService {
    Interface: <font color=Green>IDataJson</font>
    Model: featureModel
    ---
    getFeature(<font color=Green>params: IdParam</font>)
: Observable<IDataJson>
    transformFeature(<font color=Green>params:
IDataJson</font>) : featureModel
}


featureComponent --o featureRouterModule
featureModel --o featureComponent
featureModel -right-* featureService
IDataJson -left-* featureService
featureService --o featureComponent

```
```

2.   Then preview:
```

Illustration widgets

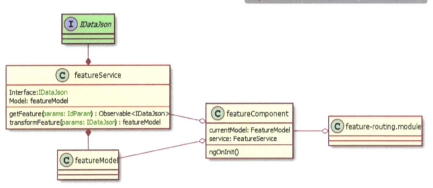

Process snippet for sequence diagrams

1. Type code source below (a full example of sequence diagram based on Angular framework)

```plantuml
'SETTINGS
'---
'scale 720 width
'left to right direction

'Title custom style
skinparam titleBorderRoundCorner 0
skinparam titleBorderThickness 1
skinparam titleBackgroundColor red
skinparam titleFontColor white
skinparam titleFontSize 24

'legend custom style
skinparam legendBorderRoundCorner 0
skinparam legendBorderThickness 0
skinparam legendFontSize 14
skinparam legendFontColor white
skinparam legendBackgroundColor darkGrey

'HEADER
'---
title
<font color=white> Frontend : Sequence diagram </font>
end title

legend top right
<font color=red>Objective : </font> Overview of the
system's process.
end legend
```

```
'BODY
'---

'custom settings
hide footbox

actor user

box "app Frontend" #lightBlue
    participant "templateView \n(router-outlet)" as
templateView <<View>>
    participant featureRouterModule <<Route>>
    participant featureComponent <<ViewModel>>
    participant featureModel <<Model>>
    participant featureService #lightGreen
    participant IdataJson  <<interface>> #lightGreen
end box


box "api Backend  \n(data or web service)" #lightGreen
    participant featureApi #lightGreen
end box

user -> templateView : Interaction
activate user
activate templateView
templateView -> featureRouterModule : Request partial
view \n and handle events
activate featureRouterModule

featureRouterModule -> featureComponent : Load
component
destroy featureRouterModule
activate featureComponent

featureComponent -> featureService : Method call service
activate featureService #lightGreen
```

featureComponent -> featureModel : Method call data
activate featureModel

featureService -[#darkGreen]> featureApi : Method call
httpClient
activate featureApi #lightGreen

featureApi -[#darkGreen]> IdataJson : Return JSON data
deactivate featureApi
activate IdataJson #lightGreen

IdataJson -[#darkGreen]> featureService : Return Object
<IdataJson>
deactivate IdataJson

featureService -[#darkGreen]> featureService :
<back:darkGreen><color:white>Adapt IdataJson for
featureModel</color></back>\n<back:darkGreen><color:whit
e>with a transform function</color></back>
activate featureService #lightGreen
deactivate featureService

featureService -[#darkGreen]> featureModel: Update
featureModel
deactivate featureService

featureModel -> featureComponent : Update data
properties

featureComponent -> templateView : Render template view
\n and Bind data properties
deactivate featureModel
deactivate featureComponent

templateView -> user : interaction

deactivate templateView
deactivate user

```

2.   Then preview:

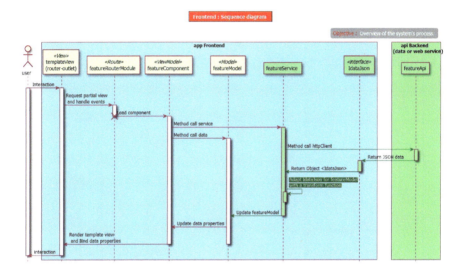

IV.   Multiple export formats

For sharing

(?) User note:

Your notes from your own practices :

....
....
....
....

Install any of the following to export to multiple formats in your preferred Markdown flavor. Markdown applications will automatically detect their installation, allowing you to export to HTML, PDF, Word, Powerpoint, EPUB, ODT, PDF and more!

- **Pandoc:** https://pandoc.org/
- **MultiMarkdown:** https://fletcherpenney.net/multimarkdown/
- **Discount:** http://www.pell.portland.or.us/~orc/Code/discount/
- **commonmark:** https://commonmark.org/

Here we will use and recommend you to install Pandoc library as full examples.

1. Pandoc, the swiss-army knife

Pandoc: https://pandoc.org/ If you need to convert files from one markup format into another, pandoc is your swiss-army knife. Pandoc can convert between the following formats:

- Lightweight markup formats
    - Markdown (including CommonMark and GitHub-flavored Markdown)
    - reStructuredText
    - AsciiDoc
    - Emacs Org-Mode
    - Emacs Muse
    - Textile
    - txt2tags
- HTML formats
    - (X)HTML 4
    - HTML5
- Ebooks
    - EPUB version 2 or 3
    - FictionBook2
- TeX formats
    - LaTeX
- XML formats
    - DocBook version 4 or 5
- PDF
    - via pdflatex, xelatex, lualatex, pdfroff, wkhtml2pdf, prince, or weasyprint.
- Slide show formats
    - LaTeX Beamer
    - Slidy
    - reveal.js
    - Slideous
    - S5
    - DZSlides
- Word processor formats
    - Microsoft Word docx
    - OpenOffice/LibreOffice ODT
    - OpenDocument XML

-     –   Microsoft PowerPoint
- Interactive notebook formats
  -   –   Jupyter notebook (ipynb)
- Page layout formats
  -   –   InDesign ICML
- Wiki markup formats
  -   –   MediaWiki markup
  -   –   DokuWiki markup
  -   –   TikiWiki markup
  -   –   TWiki markup
  -   –   Vimwiki markup
  -   –   XWiki markup
  -   –   ZimWiki markup
  -   –   Jira wiki markup

To download and install Pandoc:
https://pandoc.org/installing.html

(?) User note:

Your notes from your own practices :

....
....
....
....

2. Recommended Addons for Markdown and Pandoc

(?) User note:
Your notes from your own practices :
....
....
....
....

Markdown Preview Enhanced, Prince engine, ImageMagick engine, PlantUML filter for pandoc, some optionnal custom files for specific needs.

- **Markdown Preview Enhanced:** extension for markdown quick preview and pandoc quick render directly in the microsoft Visual Code editor. - https://marketplace.visualstudio.com/items?itemName=shd101 wyy.markdown-preview-enhanced (Include a pandoc button command) To read advanced configuration : **https://shd101wyy.github.io/markdown-preview-enhanced/#/pandoc-pdf**

- **Pandoc PlantUML Filter:** Pandoc filter for PlantUML code blocks

pandoc-plantuml-filter - https://github.com/kbonne/pandoc-plantuml-filter Needs plantuml.jar from http://plantuml.com/

1. Required: Install **Haskell** - https://www.haskell.org/downloads/

   After Haskell installation.

(i) Info note:

On Windows OS, add to the system environment variable PATH the python folder path and the PIP folder path (python subfolder Scripts).

(!) Warning note:

On Windows OS, during the writing of this book, there was still an issue (probleme of compatibility versions with pandoc). Maybe it was resolved now …

---

2. Then install the pandoc plantuml filter by following setup instructions on the README page:

- https://github.com/kbonne/pandoc-plantuml-filter

3. And use it like any other pandoc filter

> *pandoc sample.md -o sample.pdf --filter pandoc-plantuml-filter*
>
> *pandoc --from markdown --to html5 -o "sample.html" --filter pandoc-plantuml-filter "sample.md"*

- **Latex PDF engine:** By default, Pandoc creates PDFs using LaTeX. To install a basic TeX/LaTeX system **MikTex** - **https://miktex.org**

> *1. Download and install MikTex ,*
> **https://miktex.org/download**
>
> *2. On Microsoft Windows OS, add the command to environment variable system called `PATH`: for example `C:\Users\...\AppData\Local\Programs\MiKTeX 2.9\miktex\bin\x64\`*
>
> *3. then restart Visual code*

- **Prince engine:** for PDF generation By default, Pandoc creates PDFs using LaTeX. We recommend installing a more stable addon called **Prince** - **https://www.princexml.com/**

> *1. Download and install prince ,*
> **https://www.princexml.com/download/**
>
> *2. On Microsoft Windows OS, add the command to environment variable system called `PATH`: C:\Program Files (x86)\Prince\engine\bin*

3. then restart Visual code

- **ImageMagick engine:** for Convert, Edit, or Compose Bitmap Images Use ImageMagick® to create, edit, compose, and convert bitmap images. Resize an image, crop it, change its shades and colors, add captions, and more. ImageMagick - https://imagemagick.org

  1. Download and install ImageMagick ,

  https://imagemagick.org/script/download.php

  2. On Microsoft Windows OS, add the command to environment variable system called `PATH`: C:\Program Files\ImageMagick-7.0.9-Q16

  3. then restart Visual Code

(!) Warning note:

on Windows "convert.exe missing from 7.0.1-Q16?" This file has been replaced on ImageMagick latest version by magick.exe file.

So to make pandoc work again with ImageMagick, you can wait for an updated version of pandoc or duplicate the magick.exefile and rename it convert.exe file in the software folder.

Source : http://www.imagemagick.org/discourse-server/viewtopic.php?t=29582

- Optionnaly **some custom style, template and metadata files** for specifying style and contents

    - Optionnaly a **YAML or JSON metadata file** that can be named metadata.yaml for defining data options.
    - Optionnaly some **Custom style files** depending on chosen output format for defining custom graphic style.
    - Optionnaly some **Custom template files** depending on chosen output format for defining custom layout and content style.

Resume Requirements:

- **Markdown preview enhanced** extension for Microsoft Visual Code to preview and render quickly directly in visual code editor.

- **Prince** engine to convert markdown to PDF

- **ImageMagick** to convert, edit, or compose Bitmap Images https://imagemagick.org

- **Pandoc PlantUML filter** for PlantUML code blocks

- Optionnaly **some custom style, template and metadata files** for specifying style and contents

Generate a .PDF document with Pandoc

- With Markdown Preview Enhanced, you need to specify pdf_document output format and options in the front-matter of your document (the default pdf engine for pandoc is pdflatex, you can still replace it by prince engine for example):

```
---
output:
  pdf_document:
    toc: true
    toc_depth: 2
    path: ./exports/document.pdf
    latex_engine: pdflatex
    pandoc_args: ["--pdf-engine=pdflatex", "--dpi=300", "--highlight-style=tango", "--metadata=keywords:'document'"]
---
```

- Or with pandoc command line:

```
pandoc --from markdown --to html5 -o "./exports/document.pdf" --filter pandoc-plantuml-filter "sample.md" --pdf-engine pdflatex
```

> ### (!) Warning note:
>
> Markdown was originally made to be rendered on HTML output so still today depending on many factors, the render result may not look exactly as what you expected ; You will have to finalize it after render with an visual editor specific to your output type.

Generate a .DOCX word document with Pandoc

you need to specify pdf_document output format and options in the front-matter of your document:

```
---
output:
  word_document:
    toc: true
    toc_depth: 2
    path: ./exports/document.docx
    pandoc_args: ["--dpi=300", "--highlight-style=tango", --metadata=keywords:'document'"]
---
```

*   Or with pandoc command line:

```
pandoc --from markdown --to docx  -o "./exports/document.docx"  --filter pandoc-plantuml-filter "sample.md"
```

Generate an .EPUB document with Pandoc

- With Markdown Preview Enhanced, you need to specify pdf_document output format and options in the front-matter of your document:

```
---
output:
  custom_document:
    toc: true
    toc_depth: 2
    path: ./exports/document.epub
    pandoc_args: ["--dpi=300", "--highlight-style=tango","--metadata=keywords:'document'"]
---
```

- Or with pandoc command line:

```
pandoc --from markdown --to epub  -o "./exports/document.epub"  --filter pandoc-plantuml-filter "sample.md"
```

Markdown was originally made to be rendered on HTML output so still today depending on many factors, the render result may not look exactly as what you expected ; You will have to finalize it after render with an visual editor specific to your output type.

Generate an .HTML document with Pandoc

- With Markdown Preview Enhanced, you need to specify pdf_document output format and options in the front-matter of your document:

```
---
output:
  custom_document:
    toc: true
    toc_depth: 2
    path: ./exports/document.html
    pandoc_args: ["--dpi=300", "--highlight-style=tango",--
metadata=keywords:'document'"]
---
```

- Or with pandoc command line:

```
pandoc --from markdown --to html5  -o
"./exports/document.html"  --filter pandoc-plantuml-filter
"sample.md"
```

Generate a .PPTX powerpoint document with Pandoc

- With Markdown Preview Enhanced, you need to specify custom_document output format and options in the front-matter of your document:

```
---
output:
 custom_document:
   toc: true
   toc_depth: 2
   path: ./exports/document.pptx
   pandoc_args: ["--dpi=300", "--highlight-style=tango",--
metadata=keywords:'document'"]

---
```

- Or with pandoc command line:

```
pandoc --from markdown -o "./exports/document.pptx" --
filter pandoc-plantuml-filter  "sample.md"
```

(!) Warning note:

Markdown was originally made to be rendered on HTML output so still today depending on many factors, the render result may not look exactly as what you expected ; You will have to finalize it after render with an visual editor specific to your output type.

Conclusion

Resume :

Markdown, the lightweight markup language is well suited for helping write quickly and easily some documents like notes, web contents, or for helping generate print-ready documents.

But some improvements are still needed for complete and robust cross-device documentation and dynamic publication.

Oulook :

Next step would be probably to help improve all these Markdown parsers and libraries to achieve a complete entreprise-level solution on various output formats.

But today to learn more about this markup language, you can still start using it on your daily work of helping your team to gain success.

"Sometimes creativity just means the daily work of helping others to see a problem in a different way"
Joseph Badaracco

(?) User note:

Your notes from your own practices :

....
....
....
....

Appendix

Markdown Lint : Author Rules

From **MarkdownLint:**
https://github.com/DavidAnson/markdownlint

Link source:
https://github.com/DavidAnson/markdownlint/blob/master/doc/Rules.md

Acknowledgments - Reference sources

- **EasyGuide.tech:** https://easyguide.tech

- **Wikipedia:** https://en.wikipedia.org/wiki/Markdown

- **CommonMark:** https://commonmark.org/

- **Markdownguide:** https://www.markdownguide.org

- **GitHub Flavored Markdown:** https://guides.github.com/features/mastering-markdown/

- **MarkdownLint:** https://github.com/DavidAnson/markdownlint

- **Markdown Preview Enhanced** https://github.com/shd101wyy/markdown-preview-enhanced

- **PlantUML** https://github.com/plantuml/plantuml

- **Pandoc** https://github.com/jgm/pandoc

- **Babelmark 2** https://johnmacfarlane.net/babelmark2/faq.html

Licenses

Copyright (c) 2020-present Cheikhna Diouf - Cheikhnadiouf.com, contact@cheikhnadiouf.com (Cheikhnadiouf.com)

Copyright (c) 2020-present EasyGuide.tech, Inc. info@easyguide.tech (easyguide.tech)

Markdown mark

- **Markdown** was developed by John Gruber (https://daringfireball.net/projects/markdown/) in collaboration with Aaron Swartz.

- **The Markdown Mark** was designed and built by Dustin Curtis (https://dustincurtis.com). Important contributions were provided by Mac Tyler (http://mactyler.com).

- **DavidAnson/markdownlint** is licensed under the MIT License(see details online). https://github.com/DavidAnson/markdownlint

- **YiyiWang/markdown-preview-enhanced** is licensed under the University of Illinois/NCSA Open Source License (see details online). https://github.com/shd101wyy/markdown-preview-enhanced

- **JohnMacFarlane/CommonMark suits** is released under multiple licenses (see details online). https://github.com/commonmark

Appendix

- **JohnMacFarlane/Pandoc** is licensed under the GPL License with exceptions (see details online). https://github.com/jgm/pandoc

- **ArnaudRoques/plantUML** is licensed under the GNU General Public License (see details online). https://github.com/plantuml/plantuml

- **graphp/graphviz** is licensed under the MIT License (see details online). https://github.com/graphp/graphviz

- **microsoft/vscode** is licensed under the MIT License (see details online). https://github.com/Microsoft/vscode

---

- Image book cover :
  Quill pen isolated on the white background by DrazenVukelic
- Image sample : **We Are The World** album cover -
  http://usaforafrica.org/

www.ingramcontent.com/pod-product-compliance
Lightning Source LLC
Chambersburg PA
CBHW041142050326
40689CB00001B/455